2014 Mark J. Krejci, Ph.D.

Copyright © 2014 by Mark J. Krejci, Ph.D.

All rights reserved

No use of this Handbook is permitted without the express written authority of the author. This Handbook is intended only for the use of students registered in Abnormal Psychology at Concordia College, Moorhead, Minnesota. This Handbook is only to be used for educational purposes by these students. Use of the printed material in the Handbook or any material that students may insert for the diagnosis, treatment or evaluation of any actual person either in or outside of a treatment environment is <u>strictly prohibited</u>. Use of this material for entertainment purposes is also <u>strictly prohibited</u>. The author does not accept any responsibility for the use of material in this Handbook outside of the context of learning about mental illness and other related information within the context of the Abnormal Psychology course.

No parts of this Handbook may be reproduced in any fashion without the written authority of the author.

Diagnostic Titles are taken from the Diagnostic and Statistical Manual of Mental Disorders, Fifth Edition (DSM-V), © 2013 American Psychiatric Association. The limited amount of material from the DSM-V is used under the Fair Use Exemption (Title 17, U.S. Code, §107) of the U.S. Federal Copyright code.

Cover photograph is from the personal collection of the author.
The photograph is of the Imperial War Museum in London, England.

Table of Contents

1. Introduction-- 1

2. Daily Course Guide--- 3

3. On-line Lecture Guide-- 10

Lecture 1	11	Lecture 17	49
Lecture 2	15	Lecture 18	54
Lecture 3	18	Lecture 19	58
Lecture 4	20	Lecture 20	60
Lecture 5	23	Lecture 21	61
Lecture 6	24	Lecture 22	63
Lecture 7	26	Lecture 23	67
Lecture 8	28	Lecture 24	70
Lecture 9	29	Lecture 25	72
Lecture 10	31	Lecture 26	78
Lecture 11	33	Lecture 27	83
Lecture 12	36	Lecture 28	85
Lecture 13	38	Lecture 29	88
Lecture 14	40	Lecture 30	92
Lecture 15	45	Lecture 31	95
Lecture 16	46	Lecture 32	99

4. Clinical Simulation Exercise---102

5. Computer Lab Manual---107

6. Client 6 Assignment--115

7. Stress Journal-- 116

Introduction

The Abnormal Psychology Course Handbook will be used in conjunction with Abnormal Psychology at Concordia College. The handbook contains information about the course structure and schedule, exercise sheets you will need for the on-line diagnostic lectures and a description of the clinical simulation exercise that you will participate in throughout the semester.

Course Structure

The course will have the primary aim of helping you develop a sense of empathy for those who have a mental illness. To do that I believe you have to learn how to understand mental illness with both your head and your heart. By that, I mean that you need to learn about the facts of mental illness: how it is defined, what causes it, and how it is treated, but you also need to encounter the people who have the illness and who treat those coping with it.

In order to do this, you will be participating in a series of in-class and homework learning experiences. In general, they will include:

> Lectures on background, diagnostics, treatment and etiology: While some of these lectures will take part during class, a number will occur via the on-line environment. I am not using a standard Abnormal Psychology textbook for this course because they tend to contain too much information (more than what you need based on the format of this course). The books all contain diagnostic criteria and some do a pretty good job of covering etiology, but I cannot justify having you purchase a book that costs around $200 to only use about 30% of the content. This is why I created this book and the on-line lectures. As you work through the on-line lectures outside of class (in lieu of reading the textbook) I will highlight information you need to note in the lecture portion of the handbook. You will be responsible for learning and understanding this material because the exams will be primarily taken from the lecture resource.
>
> Clinical Psychology Simulation Exercise: While I will explain this in more detail later in this book, in summary you will be assigned to a "treatment team" with 5-6 of your peers. The treatment team will be given a series of clients and over the course of the semester you will diagnose, plan treatment, research background, and adjust treatment based on developments in your client's conditions. In short, I will attempt to use this series of exercises to show you how the treatment of mental illness takes place in an inpatient/outpatient setting even including the need to make a financial account of the units budget and work with insurance companies to justify your treatment approach. The group will have one final assignment – developing and presenting your own case based on a mental illness I

will assign to your group. The class will have about 6 treatment teams depending on enrollment and you will be part of one of the teams. Your performance will be based on both a group grade as well as peer-to-peer evaluation.

Background readings and case studies: I will be assigning a number of readings you can access via the Internet or some found in the course reader. You will read about success stories as well as the human tragedy associated with mental illness. For example, you will read about the person diagnosed with a psychotic disorder who goes on to win the Nobel Prize in Economics. You will also read about Dr. Peter Linnerooth – Concordia class of '92 – a Captain in the U.S. army who treated U.S. soldiers for Post Traumatic Stress Disorder (PTSD) in Iraq. You will find across the readings that there is so much we do not know about mental illness and that treatment must be personal because of the great individual differences we exhibit in our lives.

Stress Journal: Stress plays a major role in the etiology and treatment of mental illness but further it impacts everyone because we all have stress. The Diathesis-Stress model for the etiology of mental illness holds that it develops because of the intersection of stress with genetic/physiological predispositions. But most people will deal with stress and the impact of that stress will not be mental illness. For some, stress is a useful motivator that allows us to achieve goals. By setting goals in our life, we create a stress condition that we can rise to achieve or which can debilitate us. Stress impacts people both physically as well as psychologically. Whether it is stress that we bring upon ourselves or imposed on us by circumstances, it is important that we all learn to cope with stress. I have a number of things I do in order to de-escalate from stress. They include time with family, reading, exercise and prayer to name the most important positive coping mechanisms I employ but I can also eat junk-food (chips or cookies) to cope as well. What are your positive and negative stress-coping habits? The stress journal will help you identify the recurring stressors in your life as well as which coping (positive or negative) you employ.

Daily Course Guide
Tuesday/Thursday Format

DAY 1

Class: Introduction, Simulation Exercise, Clinical Simulation Development, What is Mental Illness (DSM Diagnosis)

Homework: **Lecture 1** – History of Mental Illness
History of mental illness
Philippe Pinel and moral treatment 1950 movie

DAY 2

Class: History of Mental Illness, What to do about MI today?
Clinical Simulation: What do you and others know about MI

Homework: CASE STUDIES: Chapter 2

DAY 3

Class: From Freud to CBT – Introduction to CBT (and "assembly-line" psychology?)

Homework: **Lecture 2** – Introduction to DSM
Read – CBT Therapy

DAY 4

Class: CBT therapy, Clinical Interview, Review DSM Culture and Gender
CLINICAL SIMULATION: Interview format with team member

Homework: Write report – share and grade

DAY 5

Class: Some specific assessment instruments & what does it mean to be a psychologist?
Interpreting DSM profiles

Homework: **Lecture 3:** Post-Traumatic Stress Disorder
     Lecture 4: Acute Stress Disorder
     Lecture 5: Adjustment Disorder
     CASE STUDIES Pg. 317-319
     Read: "Linerooth essay"

DAY 6

Class: Drug Treatment/ Stress Cycle / Stress & Trauma Disorders
Stress Journal Explanation and Start

Homework: Read:
    CASE STUDIES: Pg. 45-50
Homework: Stress Journal #1

DAY 7

Class: Discussion of PTSD, Reading discussion
  Clinical Simulation: Treatment Facility Orientation

Homework **Lecture 6:** Separation Anxiety
     Lecture 7: Specific Phobia
     Lecture 8: Social Anxiety
     Lecture 9: Panic Disorder
     Lecture 10: Generalized Anxiety Disorder
     CASE STUDIES: Pg. 32-38

DAY 8

Class: Review of Anxiety Disorders
    <u>Clinical Simulation</u>: Client #1/ Diagnosis and Treatment Plan

Homework   **Lecture 11:** Major Depressive Disorder
              Lecture 12: Persistent Depressive Disorder (Dysthymia)
              Lecture 13: Premenstrual Dysphoric Disorder

DAY 9

Class: Suicide, Depression, Depression Inventory
    <u>Clinical Simulation</u>: Client #1 Treatment Plan feedback

Homework
    CASE STUDIES: PG 97-113

DAY 10

Class: Review Depression Articles

Homework: **Lecture 14:** Bipolar I & Bipolar II
             Lecture 15: Cyclothymia

DAY 11

Class: Bipolar Disorders / Etiology of mood disorders
    <u>Clinical Simulation</u>: Client #1 Update, Treatment plan adjustment

Homework: CASE STUDIES: PG 113-119
    <u>Homework: Stress Journal #2</u>

DAY 12

Class: Review Case Studies
Review of "Client #6" Assignment, Group workshop, Stress diary

Homework: **Lecture 16:** Personality Disorders – Cluster A
Lecture 17: Personality Disorders – Cluster B
Lecture 18: Personality Disorders – Cluster C

DAY 13

Class: Personality – What is it and how can it become "disordered."
Clinical Simulation: Client #2 (Erin) clinical interview and treatment plan

Homework: CASE STUDIES: PG 188-216
Homework: Stress Journal #3

DAY 14

Class: Mid-semester Exam

Day 15

Class: Presentation of Client #2, Personality Disorders
Clinical Simulation: Client #2 update, Client 1 update

Homework: **Lecture 19**: Obsessive-Compulsive
Lecture 20: Body Dysmorphic
Lecture 21: Hoarding and Trichotillomania

Day 16

Class: Obsessive-Compulsive & Related Disorders
Descriptions Symptom Categories for Schizophrenia
Delusions/Hallucinations/Disorganized Thinking & Speech/ Disorganized or Abnormal Motor Behavior/Negative Symptoms

Homework: **Lecture 22:** Schizophrenia
Lecture 23: Schizophreniform, Schizoaffective, Brief Psychotic

DAY 17
Class: Review of Schizophrenia disorders
    Clinical Simulation: Client #3: Interview and treatment plan

Homework: CASE STUDIES: Pg. 80-94
    Homework: Stress Journal #4

DAY 18
Class: Etiology of Schizophrenia, Discussion ON READING
    Clinical Simulation: Update Clients 1-3

Homework: **Lecture 24:** Substance Use / Intoxication / Withdrawal
    Lecture 25: Alcohol-Related Disorders
    Lecture 26: Cannabis-Related Disorders
    Lecture 27: Substance Use – other

DAY 19
Class: The diagnosis and treatment of addiction
    Clinical Simulation:

Homework: CASE STUDIES: Pg. 156-164, 219-222

DAY 20
Class: The impact of addiction
    Clinical Simulation: Client 4 interview and treatment plan

Homework: **Lecture 28:** Intellectual Disability
    Lecture 29: Autism Spectrum
    Lecture 30: Attention-Deficit/Hyperactivity
    Homework: Stress Journal #5

DAY 21
Class: Why has the incidence of Autism Spectrum increased?
<u>Clinical Simulation</u>: Client updates

Homework: CASE STUDIES: Pg. 258-262, 293-297

DAY 22
Class: Are we overmedicating our children?
NOTE: YOUR ANSWERS FOR CLIENT #6 ARE DUE TODAY
<u>Clinical Simulation</u>: Client #5

Homework: **Lecture 31:** Eating Disorders
CASE STUDIES Pg. 173-186

Day 23
Class: Eating disorders
<u>Clinical Simulation</u>: Update Clients 1-5

Homework:

Day 24
Class: Eating Disorders and our identity
<u>Clinical Simulation</u>: Client #6 interview and treatment plan

Homework: **Lecture 32:** Dissociative Disorders

DAY 25
Class: Dissociative Disorders
<u>Clinical Simulation</u>: Client updates

Homework: CASE STUDIES Pg. 55-60 & 121-136

DAY 26
Class: Paraphilia and normality

DAY 27
Class: What we have not covered – Pt. 1
    <u>Clinical Simulation</u>: Final Client Updates

DAY 28
Class: What we have not covered – Pt. 2

On-line Lecture Guide

The following pages contain outlines of the lectures you will access on-line. The outlines are not complete so that you are able to fill in information as you listen to the lecture. The lectures typically run 10 to 15 minutes and you will want to carefully note the information on the diagnostic sheets because you will use this information as part of the Clinical Simulation exercise and your exams will be related to these criteria. The lectures can be found on the Abnormal Psychology Moodle page. You will see when you need to complete the lecture by following the daily course guide in the previous section.

Most outlines cover diagnostic criteria used by mental health professionals to define the various forms of mental illness. The diagnoses and most of the specific criteria are direct quotes taken from The Diagnostic and Statistical Manual of Mental Disorders – V (2013) published by the American Psychiatric Association. I at times will also include information regarding other factors associated with the diagnostic categories and, unless otherwise noted, this information is also taken from the DSM-V. Remember that I do not necessarily provide all of the information related to each area given that this is an undergraduate psychology class and so the information you receive in these lectures and during the course should never be used to diagnose anyone in a formal or informal situation.

Lecture #1
History of Mental Illness

Historical trends in explaining MI

1.

2.

3.

4.

5.

Demonology

Used to explained most forms of all illnesses

Treatment via Demonology

Trephining

Treatment – More Humane Ancient Example

Somatogenesis

Definition –

"4 Humors"

1.

2.

3.

4.

Middle Ages

Dualistic Heresy

Signs of witchcraft

Asylum Movement

Priory of St. Mary of Bethlehem

Philippe Pinel – Paris Asylum - La Bicetre (1793)

Pinel assigned to La Salpetrie • "A Treatise on Insanity"

Quaker – William Tuke

Conclusions

Lecture #2

DSM 5: AN INTRODUCION TO DIAGNOSTICS

What is the DSM ?

Diagnostic and Statistical Manual of Mental Disorders

DSM Series

1. DSM I – 1952

2. DSM II – 1968

3. DSM III – 1980

4. DSM III-R – 1987

5. DSM IV – 1994

6. DSMIV–TR–2000 2.

7. DSM 5 – 2013

DSM 5 Breakdown

Example of Category of MI: Depressive Disorders

Specific Example:

- 296.21 – Major Depressive Disorder, Single Episode, Mild
- 296.22 – Maj Dep Dis, Single, Moderate

DSM 5 and class

DSM 5 Changes from DSM 4-TR

2 to note

1.

2.

Lecture #3

Posttraumatic Stress Disorder (PTSD)

PTSD Symptoms

A.

    1.

    2.

    3.

    4.

B. "Intrusion symptoms"

   Definition:

    1.

    2.

    3.

    4.

C.

D.

E.

F.

Examples of Trauma
(Outside range of normal stressors)

Women - Men

Iraq & Afghanistan Veterans

Lecture #4

Acute Stress Disorder

Acute Stress vs. PTSD?

Acute Stress Disorder Symptoms

A. Exposure to:_____

   1.

   2.

   3.

   4.

B. 9 or more of the following across any of the categories

Intrusion Symptoms

    1.

    2.

    3.

    4.

Negative Mood

    5.

Dissociative Symptoms

    6.

    7.

Avoidance Symptoms

8.

9.

Arousal Symptoms

10.

11.

12.

13.

14.

C. Duration:

NOTE: specific examples of the symptoms under various categories also specific examples for PTSD

Lecture #5

Adjustment Disorder

Adjustment Disorder: General Information

1.

2.

Adjustment Disorder: Symptoms

A.

B.

    Defined by:
    -

    -

C.

D.

Adjustment Disorder: Symptoms & Bereavement

Lecture #6
Separation Anxiety Disorder

Separation Anxiety: General Information

1.

2.

Separation Anxiety: Symptoms

1. Recurrent distress when _____ or _____ separation from home or major attachment figure

    1.

    2.

    3.

    4.

    5.

    6.

    7.

    8.

2. Duration

Children

Adults

NOTE: Not only found in childhood

Lecture #7

Specific Phobia

Specific Phobia: General Information

1.

2. Subtypes:

    a.

    b.

    c.

    d.

    e.

Specific Phobia: Symptoms

1.

2.

3.

4.

5. Duration:

6.

Specific Example: AGORAPHOBIA

Treatment

1.

2.

3.

Lecture #8

Social Anxiety Disorder

Social Anxiety Disorder: General Information

Social Anxiety Disorder: Symptoms

1.

2.

3.

4.

5.

6.

7.

Social Anxiety Disorder: 1 more note

Lecture #9

Panic Disorder

Panic Disorder: General Information

Panic Disorder: Symptoms

A. Abrupt onset of panic defined by experiencing 4 or more of the following:

    1.

    2.

    3.

    4.

    5.

    6.

    7.

    8.

    9.

10.

11.

12.

13.

2. After 1 attack, 1 month or more of the following:

1.

2.

3.

4.

Lecture #10

Generalized Anxiety Disorder

Generalized Anxiety Disorder: General Information

Generalized Anxiety Disorder: Symptoms

1.

2.

3. 3 or more also evident:

    1.

    2.

3.

4.

5.

6.

4.

Generalized Anxiety Disorder: Final Point

Lecture #11
Major Depressive Disorder

Major Depressive Disorder: General Information

First of three Depressive Disorders we will consider:

   1.

   2.

   3.

Course specifiers

Major Depressive Disorder: Symptoms

A.

1.

2.

3.

4.

5.

6.

7.

8.

9.

Rule out?

Major Depressive Disorder: Gender & Culture

Major Depressive Disorder: Risk Factors

Lecture #12
Persistent Depressive Disorder

Persistent Depressive Disorder: General Information

Persistent Depressive Disorder: Symptoms

A.

B.

    1.

    2.

    3.

    4.

    5.

6.

C.

D.

E.

Lecture #13

Premenstrual Dysphoric Disorder

Premenstrual Dysphoric Disorder: General Information

Premenstrual Dysphoric Disorder: Symptoms

A.

B.

    1.

    2.

3.

4.

C.

1.

2.

3.

4.

5.

6.

7.

Premenstrual Dysphoric Disorder: Why controversy?

Lecture #14
Bipolar I and Bipolar II Disorder

Bipolar I & II: General Information

Conditions related to Bipolar I & II
    Manic Episode
    Hypomanic Episode
    Major Depressive Episode

What is Mania?

Manic Episode: Criteria

A.

    Elevated Mood:

Expansive Mood:

Goal Directed:

B. During mood disturbance outlined in A – presence of 3 or more of the following:

1.

2.

3.

4.

5.

6.

7.

C.

Hypomanic Episode: Criteria

A.

B.

C.

D.

E.

Summary:
Hypomanic not as invasive or as severe as Manic episode

Major Depressive Episode: Criteria

A.

1.

2.

3.

4.

5.

6.

7.

8.

9.

B.

Bipolar I Disorder: Symptoms

A.

Bipolar II Disorder: Symptoms

A.

B.

Lecture #15
Cyclothymic Disorder

Cyclothymic: General Information

Cyclothymic Disorder: Symptoms

A.

B.

C.

Lecture #16
Personality Disorder: Cluster A

Personality Disorder: General Information

-

-

-

-

-

Personality Disorder: Cluster A
1. Paranoid Personality Disorder
2. Schizoid Personality Disorder
3. Schizotypal Personality Dis

1. Paranoid Personality Disorder: Symptoms

A.

1.

2.

3.

4.

5.

6.

7.

2. Schizoid Personality Disorder: Symptoms
A.

1.

2.

3.

4.

5.

6.

7.

3. Schizotypal Personality Disorder: Symptoms
A.

1.

2.

3.

4.

5.

6.

7.

8.

9.

Lecture #17

Personality Disorder: Cluster B

Personality Disorder: Cluster B
1. Antisocial Personality Disorder
2. Borderline Personality Disorder
3. Histrionic Personality Disorder
4. Narcissistic Personality Disorder

1. Antisocial Personality Disorder: Symptoms

A.

    1.

    2.

    3.

    4.

    5.

    6.

    7.

2. Borderline Personality Disorder: Background

-

-

Population – 1.6 – 5.9%

Outpatient – 10% Inpatient – 20%

2. Borderline Personality Disorder: Symptoms

A.

    1.

    2.

    3.

4.

5.

6.

7.

8.

9.

3. Histrionic Personality Disorder: Symptoms

A.

1.

2.

3.

4.

5.

6.

7.

8.

4. Narcissistic Personality Disorder: Symptoms

A.

1.

2.

3.

4.

5.

6.

7.

8.

9.

Lecture #18

Personality Disorder: Cluster C

Personality Disorder: Cluster C

1. Avoidant Personality Disorder
2. Dependent Personality Disorder
3. Obsessive-Compulsive Personality Disorder

1. Avoidant Personality Disorder: Symptoms

A.

    1.

    2.

    3.

    4.

5.

6.

7.

2. Dependent Personality Disorder: Symptoms

A.

1.

2.

3.

4.

5.

6.

7.

8.

3. Obsessive-Compulsive Personality Disorder: Symptoms

A.

1.

2.

3.

4.

5.

6.

7.

8.

Lecture #19

Obsessive-Compulsive Disorder

Obsessive-Compulsive Disorder: Symptoms

A.

- Obsessions Defined (1 & 2)

    1.

    2.

- Compulsions Defined (1 & 2)

    1.

    2.

B.

Obsessive-Compulsive Disorder: Other Info

-

-

-

Lecture #20

Body Dysmorphic Disorder

Body Dysmorphic Disorder: Symptoms

A.

B.

Body Dysmorphic Disorder: General

-Male – Female

- Suicide

Lecture #21
Hoarding & Trichotillomania

Hoarding

Hoarding: Symptoms

A.

B.

C.

D.

Hoarding: General

Trichotillomania (hair pulling disorder)

Trichotillomania- Symptoms

A.

B.

C.

Trichotillomania- General

Lecture #22

Schizophrenia

GENERAL INFORMATION
General Category:
<u>Schizophrenia Spectrum and Other Psychotic Disorders</u>

GENERAL INFORMATION

Key features of Psychotic Disorders
(Details presented in class)

1.

2.

3.

4.

5.

Types of Schizo. Spectrum Disorders

1.

2.

3.

4.

5.

6.

Schizophrenia: Symptoms

A.

    1.

    2.

    3.

    4.

    5.

B.

C.

D.

E.

F.

Schizophrenia:
Course Specifiers

     1.

     2.

     3.

     4-6.

     7.

Schizophrenia: General Associated Features:

Prevalence:

Course:

Gender:

Suicide Risk:

Comorbidity

Lecture #23

Schizophreniform, Schizoaffective, Brief Psychotic

Schizophreniform: Symptoms

A.

    1.

    2.

    3.

    4.

    5.

B.

Brief Psychotic Disorder: Symptoms

A.

1.
2.
3.
4.

B.

Schizoaffective Disorder: Symptoms

A.

B.

C.

Schizoaffective Disorder: General

1.

2.

3.

4. Course:

Lecture #24

Substance Use, Intoxication Withdrawal

Substance Related Disorders: Introduction

Common Feature

2 groups

1.

2.

Substance Use Disorder:
General

1.

a.

b.

c.

d.

Substance-Induced Disorders

1.

2.

Substance Intoxication or Withdrawal
Intoxication:

Withdrawal:

Substance/Medication-Induced Mental Disorder

Lecture 25
Alcohol-Related Disorders

Alcohol-Related Disorders
1. Alcohol Use Disorder
2. Alcohol Intoxication
3. Alcohol Withdrawal

Alcohol Use Disorder: Symptoms

A.

    1.

    2.

    3.

    4.

    5.

6.

7.

8.

9.

10. Tolerance

    a.

    b.

11. Withdrawal

    a.

    b.

Alcohol Use Disorder: Other information
12-month prevalence: Defined

Alcohol Use Disorder: Other information
12-month prevalence: Youth

12-month prevalence: Adults

12-month prevalence: Adult Men

12-month prevalence: Adult Women

12-month prevalence: Adult Life-span

12-month prevalence: race/ethnic youth

12-month prevalence: race/ethnic adult

Alcohol Use Disorder: Other information
Family pattern

Alcohol Use Disorder: Other Information
Global Impact

Alcohol Intoxication:

Symptoms

A.

B.

C. One or more:

1.

2.

3.

4.

5.

6.

Alcohol Withdrawal: Symptoms

A.

B.

1.

2.

3.

4.

5.

6.

7.

8.

C.

Alcohol Intoxication & Withdrawal: Why?

Lecture 26
Cannabis-Related Disorders

Cannabis-Related Disorders
1. Cannabis Use Disorder
2. Cannabis Intoxication
3. Cannabis Withdrawal

Cannabis Use Disorder: Symptoms

A.

    1.

    2.

    3.

    4.

    5.

6.

7.

8.

9.

10.

a.

b.

11.

a.

b.

Cannabis Use Disorder: Development and course

Cannabis Use Disorder: Motivation impact

Cannabis Use Disorder: Motivation impact
Recent research example:

Cannabis Use Disorder: Motivation impact
Clinical perspective:

Cannabis Use Disorder: Other information

**Cannabis Intoxication:
Symptoms**

A.

B.

C.

    1.

2.

3.

4.

Cannabis Withdrawal: Symptoms

A.

B.

1.

2.

3.

4.

5.

6.

7.

C.

Lecture 27
Substance Disorders - Others

Other Categories of Substance-Related Disorders

1. Use, Intoxication & Withdrawal

    a.

    b.

    c.

    d.

2. Only Intoxication & Withdrawal

    a.

3. Only Use & Withdrawal

    a.

4. Only Use & Intoxication
    a.

        -

        -

        b.

Lecture 28
Intellectual Disability

Neurodevelopmental Disorders

- We will cover:
1. Intellectual Disability
2. Autism Spectrum
3. Attention Deficit/Hyperactivity

Intellectual Disability:
What's in a name

Intellectual Disability:
What's in a name—severity levels

Former term   Current term

**Intellectual Disability:
Severity Levels**
- Mild, Moderate, Severe, Profound

**Intellectual Disability:
Diagnostic Criteria**
A. Deficits in intellectual functions
B. Deficits in adaptive functions
C. Onset of A & B during the developmental period

A. Deficits in intellectual functions
    IQ Information

    Areas of deficit

Diagnosis based on ….

B. Deficits in adaptive functioning

Defined as ability for "Adaptive functioning" in society

C. Onset during developmental period

Lecture 29
Autism Spectrum Disorder

Autism "Spectrum"

**Autism Spectrum:
Diagnostic Criteria**

A.

    1.

    2.

    3.

Severity specifier:

Level 1: Requiring Support

Level 2: Requiring Substantial Support

Level 3: Requiring Very Substantial Support

B.

1.

2.

3.

4.

Severity Specifier:

Level 1: Requiring Support

Level 2: Requiring Substantial Support

Level 3: Requiring Very Substantial Support

C.

D.

E.

Autism Spectrum:
Other Information

Gender:

Genetics:

Environmental Influencers:

Course / Onset:

Lecture 30
Attention-Deficit/Hyperactivity (ADHD)

ADHD: Introduction

**ADHD:
Diagnostic Criteria**

A.

Defining Inattention

    a.

    b.

    c.

    d.

    e.

    f.

g.

h.

i.

Defining Hyperactivity/Impulsivity

a.

b.

c.

d.

e.

f.

g.

h.

i.

B.

C.

D.

ADHD:
Specify
Combined presentation

Predominately inattentive

Predominately hyperactive/impulsive

ADHD:
Other Information

Prevalence:

Gender:

Genetic:

Lecture 31
Eating Disorders
Anorexia Nervosa & Bulimia Nervosa

Eating Disorders

- Pica

- Rumination

- Avoidant/Restrictive Food Intake

- Binge-Eating

- Anorexia Nervosa

- Bulimia Nervosa

Anorexia Nervosa: Diagnostic Criteria

A.

B.

C.

Specify:

Restricting type

Binge-eating/purging type

**Anorexia Nervosa:
Other Information**

Accompanying Medical Conditions:

Gender:

Course:

Culture:

Suicide:

Bulimia Nervosa: Diagnostic Criteria

A.

   1.

   2.

B.

C.

D.

E.

**Bulimia Nervosa:
Severity**

Mild –

Moderate –

Severe –

Extreme –

**Bulimia Nervosa:
Other information**

Accompanying Medical Conditions:

Gender:

Course:

Precursor:

Lecture 32
Dissociative Disorders

Dissociative Disorders

- Dissociative Identity Disorder
- Dissociative Amnesia
- Depersonalization / Derealization Disorder

Dissociative Identity Disorder: What's in a name?

Multiple Personality Disorder

Dissociative Identity Disorder: Diagnostic Criteria

A.

B.

C.

D.

E.

Dissociative Amnesia: Diagnostic Criteria

A.

B.

C.

Depersonalization/ Derealization: Diagnostic Criteria

A. Presence of persistent or recurrent:

Depersonalization:

Derealization:

B.

C.

D.

Clinical Simulation Exercise

Mercy Hospital Mental Health Treatment Unit

Mercy Hospital of Moorhead, Minnesota, a general service hospital and clinic, provides both inpatient and outpatient mental health care through its Mental Health Treatment Unit. Mental health professionals are organized in a treatment team format with each team consisting of a Psychiatrist (MD), two Psychologists (one from the inpatient unit (IP) and one from outpatient services (OP)) a Clinical Social Worker (SW) (who follows patients across inpatient and outpatient units if inpatient hospitalization is warranted) a Lead Registered Nurse (RN), and a team Administrative Member (AM). Each treatment unit addresses the needs of many clients that are receiving inpatient care, outpatient therapy and social support, and discharge plans as warranted by the clients presenting issues and course of treatment. Dr. Mark J. Krejci, MN LP #1962 is the Chief of Mental Health Services at Mercy Hospital and is the direct supervisor of all mental health treatment teams.

Treatment Team Duties by Position

Psychiatrist: Prescribes medication as warranted by the presenting condition as well as other health conditions. Is the primary referral source for other medical consultations as needed based on client presenting general medical condition. Monitors client primarily through feedback from other members of treatment team but is available for brief medical checks.

Inpatient Psychologist: Is the primary member of the team responsible for the treatment plan for clients in inpatient care. Conducts individual and group psychotherapy in the inpatient unit with assigned clients. Is responsible for ordering and interpreting psychological assessment for inpatient clients.

Outpatient Psychologist: Is the primary member of the team responsible for the treatment plan for clients in outpatient care. When client transitions from inpatient to outpatient status, takes over therapy and treatment plan oversight from Inpatient Psychologist. Is responsible for ordering and interpreting psychological assessment for outpatient clients.

Clinical Social Worker: Meets with client to assess social/occupational functioning and required interventions. All Clinical Social Workers assigned to the Mercy Hospital psychiatric unit are AAMFT (American Association of Marriage and Family Therapists) certified and thus do all marriage and family therapy at times in conjunction with the Inpatient or Outpatient Psychologist.

Registered Nurse: The lead Registered Nurse for the treatment team develops care-plans for inpatient and outpatient clients, working with unit nurses on the psychiatric ward, community-based nurses, and/or family members to ensure that the client's medical and self-care needs are being met.

Administrative Member: Works with the client to ensure that payment obligations can be met. Will work with the client's healthcare insurance provider to maximize coverage received. Will also assist client in securing outside funds (loans) if available or, as an alternative for coverage of deductible amounts and non-covered charges, will liaison between the client and the Mercy Hospital business office to establish a payment plan. Clients who do not have their own health insurance coverage are assisted in applying for government need-based aid (Medicare) or government mandated (Affordable Care Act – Minnesota Health Cooperative) coverage. All patients must have coverage of some form in order to receive care. The Administrative Member has overall responsibility for coordinating paperwork (treatment plans and modifications).

Intake Session

During intake sessions, the treatment team will all participate in the intake interview. The initial interview will be conducted by one of the team's psychologists with other members viewing from the observation room. Treatment team members may request certain questions via the "Bug-in-the-Ear" technology. At the conclusion of the interview, the treatment team must agree on an initial diagnosis and treatment plan. Each team member then completes clinical notes within their areas and the Administrative Team Member compiles the information and completes the Mercy Hospital Psychiatric Intake and Treatment Plan form (Form found on next page – it will be e-mailed to all treatment team members.

At the conclusion of the intake session, each team must e-mail a completed Psychiatric Intake and Treatment Plan form to the director of Mental Health Services, Dr. Mark Krejci who has the final sign-off on each plan.

Weekly Care Notes

Each team will be responsible for completing a weekly care note for each client [SPECIFIC NOTES WILL BE ASSIGNED IN CLASS BASED ON UPDATES]. The Treatment Team must also keep a running budget for the care of each client.

Mercy Hospital Psychiatric Intake and Treatment Plan

Date:

Group # and Names:

General Information (SW)

Client Name:

Date of Birth/Client Age:

Marital Status:

Family Status: (indicate number, names and ages of any children)

Reason For Referral (AM)

Past Psychiatric/Medical History (IP or OP)

Insurance Coverage (AM)

Appearance (RN)

Behavior Patterns (IP or OP)

Emotion Patterns (IP or OP)

Cognition/Perception (IP or OP)

Social Work Analysis (SW)

How is the client functioning in each of the following areas – are there any specific issues related to their mental illness related to each of these areas. (If any of these areas require social work intervention make sure it(they) is(are) addressed in the treatment plan:

Living Situation:

Familial or Other Support Systems:

Social Functioning:

Occupational Functioning:

Self-Care Functioning:

Financial Functioning:

Diagnosis (Entire Team) (List diagnosis and specific symptoms recognized as part of diagnosis)

Medication Treatment (MD) (also include any other medical conditions requiring attention)

Web sites for medication:

http://www.nimh.nih.gov/health/publications/mental-health-medications/index.shtml

http://en.wikipedia.org/wiki/List_of_psychiatric_medications_by_condition_treated

http://psychcentral.com/lib/top-25-psychiatric-medication-prescriptions-for-2011/00012586

State Medication name, dose, when administered (e.g. 200 mg 3X/day) and why you selected this medication

Treatment Plan (IP or OP)
Note: if client is to receive inpatient care, the IP should develop this part and the OP should complete Behavior, Emotion and Cognition/Perception sections above. The roles are reversed if the client is to receive outpatient care.

This should include a review of the issues you plan to address in therapy including which cognitions (following CBT) you will address. You should also address the approach you would have in approaching the therapeutic issues (i.e. which comes first, second and which issues might not be immediately addressed).

If Inpatient – you should indicate how many days you believe the client will be hospitalized
If Outpatient – you should indicate how many sessions and frequency (e.g. 10 sessions, one per week followed by monthly sessions for 4 months)

Inpatient or Outpatient Nursing Care Plan (RN)

What general medical conditions need to be addressed/assessed/treated. What times will the medication be delivered. Who will deliver the medication(s). If inpatient care is provided, how will the client be transitioned towards being able to take care of his or her own medications if needed (note – inpatient care staff always keeps possession of the medication but client may be given greater responsibility for asking for medication at appropriate times).

Projected cost of treatment & payment method (AM)

A budget will need to be developed for each client. Mercy Hospital charges $1000 per day for inpatient care plus the cost of medications. This covers all cost for treatment team care.

Outpatient psychiatry is $500 per session for med-checks, $200 per hour for therapy from a psychologist, $75 per assessment given, Nursing visits cost $75 per visit, Social Work therapy contact costs $125 per hour.

Each client will come with a "fact sheet" that will detail what type of insurance coverage the person has available.

Computer Lab Manual

Clinical Diagnostic Exercise

Abnormal Psychology Computer Lab Manual

Mark J. Krejci, Ph.D.
Sara Christianson
Andrew Kollar

Concordia College

This project was funded, in part, by a
Centennial Scholars Classroom Grant
from
Concordia College
Moorhead, Minnesota

Summer, 2001

© Mark Krejci 2001

INTRODUCTION

This computer lab simulates a clinical intake interview. As you learned in class, many mental health centers assign new clients to a therapist (as part of a treatment team) who conducts a clinical interview. The psychologist is to complete an interview that allows the team to identify any appropriate diagnosis as well as understand the client's view of the world and of himself or herself. The team then writes a clinical interview report that is given to the therapist assigned to the case or, as is set-up at Mercy Hospital, the interview report also includes an initial treatment plan.

The lab experience allows you to interview a client as if you were the conducting an intake interview. You will be assigned a client at different points in the semester and access the lab through the Abnormal Psychology web page. During the interview, you will pick from a menu of 100 questions and get to know the client. After you have completed the interview, you will be expected to complete the assigned clinical report.

HOW TO OPERATE THE LAB

You will be given instructions in class on how to locate the Abnormal Psychology Web Page. When you first access the lab, read the first page before proceeding. One thing you will note is that the "clients" are played by role-play volunteers. The authors wish to thank these volunteers for making this lab experience possible.

You start the interview by clicking on the name of the assigned client. The first screen is composed of three windows. In the upper right is a picture of the client you will be interviewing. The upper left window contains the client's intake form. The appointment secretary completed this intake form when the client called to make the appointment. The appointment secretary has checked the accuracy of the information when the client arrived for the appointment. Take time to scan through the intake information.

You are now ready to ask questions. In the bottom window is a grid containing the numbers 1 through 100. These numbers correspond to the questions listed in Appendix A. By clicking on a number, you are in effect asking the client that question.

The panel is color-coded with a certain color representing a certain category of question. The categories are:

Introduction - Yellow   Background - Green
Behavior - Orange   Affect - Red
Perception - Dark Blue   Reality Orientation - Blue Green
Cognitive Abilities - Light Purple   Anxiety/Stress - Dark Purple
Interpersonal Relationships - Violet

When you click on one of the question numbers, you should see the video clip appear and played by the default media player.

NOTES ON COMPUTER OPERATION

-- If you are asked if you should download the video clip - select the "NO" option. This will greatly speed up the process and not fill the computer's memory. Most Concordia College computers will not offer this option but if you do this lab on your own computer you may run into this trouble. Also, when the clip is completed, close the media player so that numerous media players' windows are not opened filling your computer's memory.

-- SINGLE CLICK the questions. If you "double-click" the question button, you may receive a message that the audio cannot be heard. After the clip has played, single-click the question again and the audio should play without problem.

You should ask questions to accomplish 2 purposes:

1. Identify the client's mental illness

and

2. Get to know the client's perspective on his or her life

Sometimes the diagnosis will be easy to identify and other times more difficult. After you have completed asking your questions click the Assessment link found under the question grid for more information on further assessment results and consultations with other professionals.

CLINICAL NOTES

During the clinical interview, you will want to keep notes so that you can remember the information for the clinical report. Make sure to record needed information from the client's intake form as well as information from his or her responses. Some clinicians keep notes during the clinical interview while others record notes as soon as the interview is completed. However you decide to proceed, it is highly recommended that you write some notes before writing your clinical report.

ACKNOWLEDGEMENTS

This lab was supported, in part, by a Centennial Scholars Classroom Grant received from Concordia College in Moorhead Minnesota. The authors wish to thank the college for its support. We would also like to thank the volunteers who served as the role-play clients. The hours that were put into the taping sessions went well because of their concentration and hard work. We would also like to thank Dr. Krejci's two co-authors of the first version of this lab experience. The first version was completely based on text presentation of the client and was put together by Dr. Mark Krejci and students Maria Sather and David Reich in 1988. It was our desire back then to have a video and audio presentation of the clients, but the technology was available at the time. Finally, Dr. Krejci would like to thank the hundreds of students who have completed the first version of the lab and gave valuable feedback on the utility of the experience in their learning and later in their professional lives.

APPENDIX A

CLINICAL INTERVIEW QUESTIONS

INTRODUCTION (Yellow)
1. Hello, we will be talking for a while today. (you extend your hand to shake hands with client). To begin with, tell me about why you are here?

BACKGROUND AND APPEARANCE (Green)
2. Tell me about your family?
3. Tell me about your life when you were a child or adolescent?
4. How is your relationship with your spouse (the person you are dating)?
5. (if the client was divorced) Tell me about your first marriage and why did it end?
6. What did/do you think of school?
7. Tell me about your employment history?
8. Tell me about any problems you have had with your past or present jobs?
9. Have you ever broken the law?
10. Have you ever been told you have a mental illness?
11. Have you ever seen a counselor/psychologist before?
12. Have you ever been on any medications for mental illness?
13. Is your appearance (or fashion) important to you?

BEHAVIOR (Orange)
14. What do you enjoy doing during your free time?
15. What things get you excited?
16. Are you able to relax?
17. Have you ever experienced times when you felt really energized and got a lot of things done?
18. Have you ever gone on buying sprees?
19. Do you have as much energy now as you once did?
20. Have you lost interest in any activities that you previously enjoyed?
21. Tell me about times when you find yourself talking much of the time?
22. Are you healthy?
23. Do you experience any tension in your body?
24. Does your heart ever seem to pound especially hard or do you ever have trouble breathing?
25. Do you have any difficulties sleeping?
26. Has you appetite changed recently?
27. Are you happy with your body weight?
28. Have you ever eaten large amounts of food, perhaps even when you weren't hungry?
29. Do people talk to you about your eating habits?

30. Do you ever vomit or use laxatives to loose weight?
31. Have you ever attempted suicide or are you thinking about suicide?
32. What kinds of lies have you told?
33. Have you ever attempted to physically hurt a person?
34. Do you drink alcohol or use illegal drugs?
35. What kind and how much alcohol or illegal drugs do you use?
36. Do you ever find yourself drinking more (taking more drugs) than you wanted to?
37. Have you ever tried to stop or cut down your drinking (drug use)? (if yes) How did
    that go?
38. Have you ever missed work/school because you were hung-over, drunk, or high?
39. Do you find yourself needing more alcohol (drugs) to get drunk (high)? How much
    more?
40. Have you ever suffered from shaking, sweating, racing heart, anxiety or
    insomnia after using drugs or alcohol?

AFFECT (Red)
41. Do you feel on edge?
42. What makes you irritated?
43. Do you ever get angry? About what?
44. What makes you happy?
45. How do you feel right now?
46. How do you feel most of the time?
47. Tell me about times when you feel uncomfortable?
48. Tell me about times when you felt depressed or do you feel depressed now?
49. Tell me about the times you get upset?
50. Tell me what makes you afraid?
51. How do your feelings affect your body?
52. When feeling a certain way, do you have changes in your eating/drinking?

PERCEPTION (Dark Blue)
53. What do you think about yourself?
54. Tell me about the things you would like to change about yourself?
55. Do you hear things or see things other people don't hear or see?
56. Tell me about the things you see or hear that other people do not?
57. How long have you heard these things (or seen these things)?
*58. Do you find yourself thinking things others do not?
59. Have you ever thought things that other people did not think were true?
60. Do you ever feel that other people have control over you?
61. Do other people ever place thoughts in your mind?
62. Can you influence the minds of others?
63. Have you ever thought that certain things have special meaning just for you?
*64. How do other people treat you?

65. What qualities do you think other people admire in you?
66. What would other people change in you if they could?
67. Do you ever think that people are plotting against you?
68. Tell me about the times when you did important things.
69. Have there ever been times when you have done something important that other people did not recognize?
70. What is it like for you to be with a group of people?
71. Tell me about the times you are by yourself?
72. Tell me about how you make friends.
73. When people talk about you, what do they say?

REALITY ORIENTATION (Blue-Green)
74. What is your name and age?
75. Where are you now, what is the name of this place?
76. What is today's day of the week and date?
77. Is there anything wrong with you now?

THINKING-COGNITIVE ABILITIES (Light Purple)
78. What is the name of this state?
79. How much is 15 plus 9?
80. Repeat these numbers after me: 7, 4, 1.
81. Repeat these numbers after me: 4, 2, 7, 5.
82. Repeat these numbers after me: 9, 6, 2, 7, 1.
83. Now, I will say more numbers, but this time when I am through, I want you to say them backwards: 5, 8, 6.
84. (same task as in 83) 4, 6, 1, 9.
85. (same task as in 83) 1, 3, 7, 4.
86. Who wrote Hamlet? Shakespeare
87. Whose name is associated with the Theory of Relativity? Einstein's
88. Tell me the meaning of this saying, "Those in glass houses should not throw stones."
89. Tell me the meaning of this saying, "A stitch in time saves nine."

THINKING-ANXIETY/STRESS (Dark Purple)
90. Do you think you expect too much out of yourself?
91. When your mind is worrying, what are you thinking about?
92. Do you feel you are in control of your life?
93. What kinds of things worry you?
94. Do you ever feel the demands of your job are too much?

INTERPERSONAL (Violet)
95. Do you prefer working in a group or by yourself?
96. What qualities do you look for in a friend?
97. What role do your friends play in your life?
98. Are you having any difficulties with your family or friends or co-workers?

99. How do other people affect how you feel?
100. Do you find yourself losing contact with family and/or friends?

Client #6 Assignment

Each treatment team will be assigned a mental illness and be expected to develop a comprehensive review of the mental illness as well as develop a fictitious client for a new computer lab module. This will require that the group develop a fictitious name and background for a person with the mental illness they have been assigned and then proceed to develop the intake form as well as answers to each of the 100 questions in the computer lab. Final reports should be completed in the following order covering information related to the mental illness in each of these areas.

Treatment Team # and Names:

1. Assigned Mental Illness

2. Names of treatment team

3. List of all diagnostic criteria for the illness

4. Information on familial, gender and racial patterns found for this illness

5. Library research indicating the etiology of this mental illness (this is a mini-paper of 4-5 pages with references – place references for sections 5&6 at end of each section).

6. Library research indicating treatment of this mental illness (a second mini-paper of 4-5 pages with references).

7. A detailed outline of one specific article related to the treatment and another on the etiology of this mental illness (published in last 5 years). This section should include a review of the introduction, methodology, results and conclusions found in this article and follow this format:

    A. Title, reference information (year, journal name, volume, pages)
    B. List of Authors
    C. Summary of introduction (1 – 2 paragraphs)
    D. Summary of methodology (1 – 2 paragraphs)
    E. Summary of findings

8. Description of your fictitious client including completed intake form

9. Answers to each of the 100 questions (NOTE: type the question number followed by the client's response – for example:
    1. I am fine (write in parenthesis any behaviors the actor should display)
NOTE: Identify the questions with diagnostic significance in bold type.

Stress Journal

The stress journal will be a self-reflection on your level of stress as well as the stress-coping mechanisms you employed to deal with the stress. Many people allow stress to accumulate without taking any specific behavior to either "inoculate" themself from stress or, after experiencing a stressful event or series of events, taking steps to alleviate the impact of the stress. These exercises are to be completed by the listed dates following the format below. Remember that these will be shared with your classmates and I will read them as well and so keep this in mind as you decide what to put in your journal. You may have some things that occur that are very stressful but you may decide that you do not want to share the event with anyone in class. There is no expectation that you will share every stressful thing in your life – that is not the point of the exercise. The point of this assignment is for you to review not only the stress in your life but also how you are coping with stress.

<u>Stress Journal Format</u>

Date of the event:

Event that created stress:

>How was this event not anticipated?

>How did this event interfere with your ability to predict what was going to happen in your life?

What had you done in the previous 24 hours to inoculate yourself from stress?

What did you do after the stressful event to dissipate the stress?

>Was this a healthy (consult list provided) or unhealthy stress-coping activity?

Made in the USA
Las Vegas, NV
09 January 2021